THE ESSENTIAL BOOK OF

Glamour
and
Beauty
Spells and Magic

Beatrice Aurelia Crowley

Erebus Society

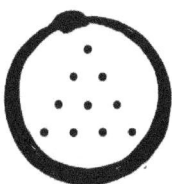

Erebus Society

First published in Great Britain in 2025
Erebus Society

First Edition

ISBN: 978-1-912461-71-4

www.ErebusSociety.com

Table of Contens

What is Glamour and Beauty Magic?

Glamour and beauty magic represent one of the most captivating and fascinating forms of spellcraft. Crafted from elements of deception, self-empowerment, and divine energy, these spells have historically been employed by witches, mystics, and enchantresses to fascinate, transform, and emanate power.

These types of magic transcend superficial charm; they embody inner strength, self-assurance, and the capacity to shape perception. Practicing them enables one to harness the intangible, manipulate energy, and embody a persona that radiates magnetism, charm, and allure.

What is this phenomenon, and how can it be integrated into the fabric of daily existence? Let us explore the essence of glamour and beauty, revealing its roots, techniques, and boundless possibilities.

UNDERSTANDING GLAMOUR AND BEAUTY MAGIC

The Essence of Glamour

Glamour magic fundamentally involves the manipulation of perception. Its origins can be traced to the archaic Scottish term "glamer," which denotes a spell that obscures reality, causing something—or someone—to seem different from its actual form.

In contrast to transformational magic that physically modifies the body, glamour magic operates through illusion and persuasion. It does not alter reality, but rather distorts others' perceptions of it. By means of intention, energy manipulation, and mystical instruments, a witch can emanate an aura of allure, self-assurance, and magnetism—whether to captivate, intrigue, or command focus.

A skilfully executed enchantment may:

❀ Augment natural attributes, rendering them more luminous or alluring.

❀ Alter the energy one radiates, rendering them captivating, mysterious, or inaccessible.

❀ Enshroud the practitioner in enigma, prompting others to disregard or overlook them at will.

❀ Evoke trust, admiration, or attraction through dynamic projection.

The Power of Beauty Magic

Glamour magic modifies perception, but beauty magic amplifies existing attributes. This type of magic is very personal and transformative, assisting practitioners in fostering self-love, confidence, and well-being.

Beauty magic is harmonising the inner self with an exterior radiance, rather than according to societal standards. Numerous spells within this tradition summon divine energies, invoking deities such as Aphrodite, Hathor, Oshun, and Brigid to provide the practitioner with brilliance, charm, and elegance.

Beauty rituals may encompass:

❀ Herbal and floral-infused ritual baths for purification and radiance enhancement.

❀ Ritualistic spells employing oils and balms to sanctify the skin and hair.

❀ Mirror work, in which affirmations and incantations alter self-perception.

❀ Aura augmentation involves the practitioner's energy field being imbued with brightness, magnetism, and attraction.

❀ At its core, beauty magic represents an act of self-admiration—a means to manifest divine luminosity and realise the most empowered iteration of oneself.

Essential Components of Glamour and Beauty Magic

1. Intent and Visualisation

All magic commences with purpose. A glamour spell lacking a definite objective is simply a hollow illusion. The witch must initially determine:

❀ Do they desire to seem more captivating, self-assured, or otherworldly?

❀ Should they exude an aura of enigma, peril, or charm?

❀ Are they pursuing invisibility, security, or dominance within a space?

Through visualisation, the intended energy is integrated into reality. A practitioner may conceive a radiant light of beauty, a veil of nebulous obscurity, or an aura of compelling allure.

2. Instruments and Components

Glamour and beauty spells frequently utilise both physical and metaphorical instruments to ground energy, including:

❀ Mirrors — Vessels of reflection and personal metamorphosis.

❀ Candles — Coloured flames to amplify particular energies (e.g., pink for self-love, gold for brilliance).

❀ Crystals: rose quartz for beauty, amethyst for mystique, and carnelian for confidence.

❀ Herbs — Chamomile for a gentle radiance, basil for appeal, and cinnamon for passionate attraction.

❀ Oils and Perfumes — Jasmine for allure, vanilla for comfort, and sandalwood for enigma.

3. Ceremonies and Incantations

Enchantments are frequently articulated in rhyme or poetic structure to imbue words with power. For Example:

"Through rose and dew, under moonlight's radiance, allow beauty to illuminate, permitting my brilliance to be observed."

Chants enhance the spell's intent and are imbued with breath, voice, and volition.

4. Natural Components

Spells for glamour and beauty frequently utilise the elements of nature.

❀ Water - Utilised in beauty baths and anointing ceremonies.

❀ Fire - Candles to evoke passion, confidence, and charisma.

❀ Earth – Crystals and botanicals to stabilise and amplify beauty.

❀ Air - Incense and fragrances to enhance one's allure.

5. Sacred Summoning

Numerous beauty rituals invoke goddesses and spirits linked to love and enchantment, including:

❀ Aphrodite (Greek) - Aesthetic allure, affection, and captivating charisma.

❀ Hathor (Egyptian) - Exuberance, sensuality, and embellishment.

❀ Oshun (Yoruba) — Affection, self-esteem, and golden luminosity.

❀ Freya (Norse) - Fortitude, allure, and authority.

❀ Floral, honey, and perfumery offerings may be presented in return for their blessings and guidance.

ORIGINS AND LORE OF GLAMOUR AND BEAUTY MAGIC

The Ancient Roots of Beauty and Illusion

Since antiquity, beauty and magic have been intricately linked, one mirroring the other in the luminous realms of myth, ritual, and metamorphosis. From the opulent chambers of Aphrodite's temple to the illuminated glades where Celtic priestesses cast spells, beauty magic transcends mere embellishment; it embodies a potent force of allure and deception.

Throughout various cultures and eras, witches, mystics, and priestesses have employed beauty magic to augment their allure and to enchant, beguile, and occasionally mislead others. Through holy oils, whispered incantations, and the blessings of celestial entities, glamour and beauty magic have influenced the fates of kings, the aspirations of lovers, and the legacies of enchantresses whose names endure in tradition.

Where did this magic originate, and how has it developed throughout time?

Ancient Egypt:

In Ancient Egypt, beauty transcended ordinary aesthetics; it represented divine equilibrium and spiritual fortitude. The Egyptians perceived beauty as a manifestation of Ma'at, the principle of harmony, truth, and order. Maintaining beauty involves harmonising with the cosmic flow, thereby attracting favour, love, and divine protection.

The Magic of Hathor: Deity of Beauty and Joy

Hathor, the luminous goddess of love, beauty, and music, was venerated by people who pursued charm, enticement, and delight. She was the matron of embellishment, prompting ceremonies in which her followers perfumed their bodies with fragrant perfumes, decorated themselves with gold, and immersed in lotus-infused waters.

5

The beautification rituals of the Egyptians frequently encompassed:

Kohl eyeliner serves not only as an embellishment but also as a talisman against the Evil Eye.

Henna tattoos are employed to encourage luck, fertility, and sensuality. Fragrant oils, like myrrh and frankincense, possess enchantments that attract lovers, augment allure, and sanctify the spirit.

Mirror scrying involves practitioners gazing into polished bronze or obsidian mirrors while reciting incantations to invoke glimpses of their ideal selves. The priests and priestesses of Hathor performed intricate ceremonies in which devotees danced, chanted, and consumed spiced wines, believing that joy constituted a spell of attraction—an expression of inner beauty.

Greek and Roman Influence:

The ancient Greeks and Romans elevated beauty magic to epic proportions, integrating it into goddess worship, poetry, and enchantment.

Aphrodite and Venus: The Pinnacle of Beauty Magic

Aphrodite (known as Venus to the Romans), the goddess of love and allure, was reputed to possess a magical girdle (cestus) that rendered her utterly seductive. Individuals desiring to emulate her charm resorted to religious rituals, seeking her favour through:

❁ Rose water baths are thought to enhance skin softness and provide an ethereal radiance upon the bather.

❁ Honey and milk masks, attributed to Venus, promote youthfulness and allure.

❁ Mirror magic, in which practitioners utilised reflections to articulate affirmations of beauty and strength.

❁ Ritual perfumes, infused with cinnamon, myrtle, and saffron, designed to attract lovers and ignite passion.

Greek courtesans, referred to as hetairai, were adept in the art of glamour magic, employing fragrances, poetry, and spellcraft to entice, captivate, and exert influence on the powerful. They recognised that beauty was both an artistic expression and a mechanism of influence.

Simultaneously, Roman women presented sacrifices at the temples of Venus, murmuring incantations over combs, mirrors, and clothes, convinced that invoking her would bestow upon them her divine luminosity.

Celtic Traditions

For the Celts, the enchantment of beauty was profoundly connected to nature, the spirits, and the mystical powers of water. In contrast to the organised glamour magic of Egypt and Rome, Celtic beauty rites were frequently conducted in lonely woodlands, moonlit lakes, and mist-shrouded hills.

Brigid: Goddess of Radiance and Rejuvenation

Brigid, the deity of healing, poetry, and beauty, was thought to bestow blessings onto individuals who pursued inner and exterior luminosity.

The Celts revered her by:

❀ Immersing oneself in sacred wells, where prayers for vitality, insight, and affection were spoken.

❀ Consuming charmed herbal infusions, typically composed of elderflower, vervain, and chamomile, to restore health and augment vitality. Reciting poetry incantations, certain that language possessed the power of metamorphosis.

Beauty rituals were frequently conducted at Beltaine and Samhain, when the barrier between realms was most tenuous, enabling mortals to acquire the charm of faerie beings. The Fair Folk were infamous for their use of glamour, presenting themselves as either extraordinarily beautiful or profoundly scary at will.

Numerous Celtic witches had the belief that authentic beauty magic emanated from within; that embodying boldness, freedom, and joy constituted the supreme enchantment.

Medieval and Renaissance Europe:

In the Mediaeval and Renaissance eras, glamour magic became increasingly clandestine, frequently concealed within alchemical manuscripts and murmured incantations.

WITCHCRAFT AND THE FEAR OF GLAMOUR

The term "glamour," as we understand it today, originated during this period, first signifying a spell capable of misleading the senses.

Witches were thought to:

❁ Obscure their genuine visage, presenting as youthful and luminous using magical means.

❁ Enchant admirers with scented potions and captivating gazes.

❁ Conjure spectral phantoms, altering their shape to evade apprehension or entice the unsuspecting.

Numerous mediaeval women were charged with sorcery solely due to their exceptional beauty or charm, reflecting the persistent fear and influence of beauty magic.

ALCHEMY AND THE QUEST FOR THE ELIXIR OF YOUTH

Alchemists and practitioners of folk magic pursued the "Elixir of Eternal Beauty," employing combinations of:

❉ Rose water for purification.

❉ Gold dust to mirror celestial luminosity.

❉ Pearl powder for luminescence enhancement.

❉ The Renaissance witnessed a resurgence of beauty to its celestial status, as queens and courtesans sought the counsel of astrologers, potion-makers, and clandestine grimoires to preserve their allure.

LEGENDS AND LORE

Morgan le Fay: The Bewitching Sorceress

In Arthurian mythology, Morgan le Fay was reputed to wield glamour magic, either as an ethereal beauty or a dark crone at her discretion. She recognised that genuine power resides in perception—a principle every glamour witch ought to retain.

The Fairy Queen and the Influence of Glamour

Fairies were adept at illusion, capable of enchanting mortals with a mere glimmer of beauty. To obtain their magic, one must present sacrifices of honey, milk, and silver; otherwise, they may revoke their gift, resulting in mere illusion.

Modern Practices:

Currently, the realms of glamour and beauty enchantment persist in their evolution, integrating ancient knowledge with modern witchcraft. Practitioners now utilise:

❀ Crystals: rose quartz for affection, moonstone for luminosity.

❀ Digital sigils imbued with beauty, confidence, and charisma.

❀ New Moon glamour rituals, establishing intentions for internal and external transformation.

Contemporary witches perceive glamour not solely as an illusion but as a means of self-empowerment—a method to harness divine beauty, confidence, and allure.

Magical Correspondences

These herbs and crystals function as potent instruments in blessing, cleansing, and purification magic, guaranteeing that energy remains harmonious, clear, and safeguarded. Utilised in ritual baths, space purification, anointing oils, or energy practices, they serve as holy allies in re-establishing equilibrium and attracting divine favour.

HERBS

ANGELICA

Enhances divine beauty and creates an aura of grace and charm, while also providing spiritual protection.

BASIL

A powerful herb for attractiveness and self-confidence, used in beauty baths and love charms.

BAY LAUREL

Used for youthfulness, wisdom, and regal presence, bestows an air of majesty and allure.

CALENDULA

(Marigold)

Enhances radiance and warmth, creating a glowing, sun-kissed energy around the practitioner.

CATNIP

Infused with feline grace and irresistible charm, enhances flirtation and playful attraction.

CHAMOMILE

A soothing herb that promotes inner peace and outer radiance, softens one's energy to appear more welcoming.

CINNAMON

Adds fire and passion to one's aura, making one appear more seductive and captivating.

CLOVE

Strengthens personal magnetism and charm, often used in enchantments for irresistible beauty.

DAMIANA

A potent herb for sensuality, confidence, and attraction, used in glamour potions and baths.

ELDERFLOWER

Associated with ethereal beauty and enchantment, often used to soften features and enhance grace.

HIBISCUS

A love-drawing herb that boosts passionate beauty and enhances one's allure.

HONEYSUCKLE

Attracts admiration, good fortune, and lasting beauty, used in perfumes and beauty charms.

JASMINE

Sacred to Aphrodite and Venus, this fragrant flower enhances sensuality, romance, and grace.

LAVENDER

Promotes grace, elegance, and inner tranquility, allowing one's natural beauty to shine.

LEMON BALM

Brightens energy and complexion, bringing clarity, youthfulness, and joy to one's presence.

MINT

Stimulates vibrancy, freshness, and attraction, used to enhance charisma and personal magnetism.

ROSE

The ultimate symbol of love and beauty, used in potions, baths, and perfumes to create radiant allure.

ROSEMARY

Increases confidence and sharpness of mind, often used to enhance memory and captivating speech.

SAFFRON

A rare and luxurious herb that bestows royal beauty, sensuality, and an air of mystery.

VANILLA

Adds warmth and sweetness to one's aura, making one appear approachable, charming, and deeply desirable.

CRYSTALS AND MINERALS

AMBER

Radiates golden warmth and youthful energy, enhancing natural glow and attraction.

AMETHYST

Provides an aura of mystery and sophistication, enhancing both beauty and spiritual wisdom.

APATITE

(Blue or Green)

Enhances confidence, charm, and clarity, helping one speak and move with grace.

AQUAMARINE

Evokes timeless beauty and elegance, enhancing feminine grace and serenity.

CARNELIAN

Boosts passion, confidence, and sensuality, making one appear more vibrant and irresistible.

CELESTITE

Creates a soft, angelic glow, best for ethereal beauty and otherworldly charm.

CITRINE

Enhances joy, radiance, and a sun-kissed glow, drawing admiration and attraction.

CLEAR QUARTZ

Amplifies any glamour or beauty spell, heightening the aura and magnifying intentions.

EMERALD

Bestows regal beauty and presence, enhances natural attractiveness and personal charm.

FLUORITE

(Purple or Green)

Creates an aura of enchantment, bringing grace and elegance to movement and speech.

GARNET

Intensifies sensuality and confidence, making one appear more alluring and magnetic.

JADE

(Green or White)

Symbolizes eternal youth and graceful beauty, enhances harmony and poise.

LABRADORITE

The stone of mystical allure, creates an ethereal glow and makes one appear enigmatic and mesmerizing.

LAPIS LAZULI

Embodies sophistication, intelligence, and royal presence, enhancing one's magnetism and confidence.

MOONSTONE

Evokes soft, feminine beauty and emotional balance, making one appear serene and enchanting.

OBSIDIAN

(Golden Sheen or Snowflake)

Binds mystery and depth to one's appearance, drawing others in with an air of intrigue.

OPAL

Bestows a shifting, almost hypnotic beauty, making one appear captivating and otherworldly.

PEARL

The stone of classic elegance and purity, perfect for refined beauty and soft radiance.

RHODONITE

Encourages self-love and emotional beauty, ensuring inner radiance shines outward.

ROSE QUARTZ

The ultimate crystal of love and beauty, enhances self-acceptance, charm, and graceful allure.

Spells

Aphrodite's Magic Mirror Bath

This magical bath ritual calls upon Aphrodite's ability to improve your beauty, appeal, and magnetic attraction. Usually under a waxing moon or when the sun or moon is in Libra or Taurus, this charm will fill you with the grace and allure of the goddess performed on a Friday, the day holy to Venus.

REQUIREMENTS:

❀ Pale green candles
❀ A single red rose
❀ Myrtle oil
❀ Clover oil
❀ One cup of sugar
❀ One cup of pink wine
❀ A dash of sandalwood perfume
❀ A natural boar-bristle brush
❀ Emerald or turquoise jewelry

Timing:

Perform this spell on a Friday at 7:00 PM. Select a night when the moon is waxing, or the sun or moon is in Libra or Taurus for added potency.

INSTRUCTIONS:

Decorate your bathroom with pale green candles and a single red rose. Create a serene and romantic atmosphere to honor Venus.

Fill the tub with hot water, as warm as you can comfortably stand.

Add a mixture of myrtle oil and clover oil to the bathwater to honor Venus.

Add one cup of sugar for sweetness.

Add one cup of pink wine for intoxication and allure.

Add a dash of sandalwood perfume for its enchanting fragrance.

Step into the bath and immerse yourself. Allow the warm, fragrant water to envelop you. Take your time to relax and unwind, enjoying a special facial treatment if desired.

After bathing, dry your hair. Perform the old hundred strokes hair-brushing routine with a magical twist:

Let your hair hang down before you.

Sweep a natural boar-bristle brush from your scalp to the ends of your hair.

As you brush, have your hand follow the brush, imagining that you are infusing your hair with power and magnetic attraction.

With each stroke, chant:

> "With every brush, my beauty grows,
> Venus' charm in my hair flows.
> Magnetic allure, by my decree,
> Beauty and love come to me."

Make yourself comfortable and take several deep, relaxing breaths. Surround yourself with vibrant green light, picturing yourself as a beautiful, radiant being. Fully immerse in this image, knowing that this is your magical self. Visualize and affirm:

> "I am beauty, I am grace,
> By Venus' power, I embrace.
> As I see, so shall I be,
> Beauty and love, come to me."

After your visualization, dress in your finest clothes. Adorn yourself with emerald or turquoise jewelry, stones sacred to Venus, for extra luck in love.

Now that you are filled with the energy of Venus and Aphrodite, step out into the world with confidence and charm. Let the magic of the spell enhance your natural beauty and attract love into your life.

Appear Less Popular

This spell is meant to metaphorically dull someone's image, therefore stripping away their social appeal and attractiveness by painting a vivid picture of the individual and then covering it with black and white chalk.

REQUIREMENTS:

❀ Black chalk
❀ Orange chalk
❀ Red chalk
❀ White chalk
❀ Yellow chalk

INSTRUCTIONS:

Perform this spell at the target's house. Select a spot on their sidewalk or the street in front of their home where you can draw without interruptions.

Begin by drawing a colorful image of the person using the orange, red, and yellow chalk. Focus on capturing their likeness with as much detail as possible. This initial vibrant image represents their current popularity and charm.

Once the colorful image is complete, use the black and white chalk to dull the picture, removing details and glamour. As you do this, chant:

> "From the picture, from the soul,
> I strip away your glamour whole.
> Colors fade, charm no more,
> Now you'll be a simple bore."

As you draw over the image, visualize the person's social allure diminishing, becoming less noticeable and attractive to others.

Step back and look at the altered image. See the person in your mind's eye as less glamorous and less popular.

Close your eyes and say:

> "By chalk and art, your charm I drain,
> Until this image fades in rain.
> As I will, so mote it be,
> Your popularity ceases to be."

Appear More Popular

REQUIREMENTS:

* Black chalk
* Orange chalk
* Red chalk
* White chalk
* Yellow chalk

INSTRUCTIONS:

Perform this spell at the target's house. Choose a spot on their sidewalk or the street in front of their home where you can draw without interruptions.

Begin by drawing the person's outline with the white and black chalk. Focus on capturing their likeness as accurately as possible.

Use the red, orange, and yellow chalk to add details to the drawing. As you do this, visualize the person becoming more glamorous and socially magnetic. Say the following incantation:

> "With this chalk and with my hands,
> I draw the lines which I demand.
> Make their face of style and grace,
> From head to toe, let beauty embrace.
> With every color, charm enhance,
> Let their presence make hearts dance."

As you draw, keep your intention clear and focused on improving the person's social appeal. Imagine the colors infusing the person with confidence and charm.

Once the drawing is complete, stand back and visualize the person becoming more popular and glamorous. See them shining brightly in social situations, attracting positive attention and admiration.

Close your eyes and say:

"By the colors bright and bold,
Their story of charm is now told.
Until this image fades away,
Their popularity will hold sway.
As I will it, so shall it be,
Popular and admired, let them be."

Appear Like a Different Person

This strong glamour spell is meant to momentarily change your look so you might seem like another person. Using the components of light, clarity, and transformation can help you to provide a fresh picture of yourself.

REQUIREMENTS:

❁ A hand mirror
❁ A white candle
❁ A small piece of clear quartz
❁ Lavender oil
❁ A piece of parchment
❁ A black pen
❁ A bowl of water
❁ Fresh mint leaves

INSTRUCTIONS:

Find a quiet and undisturbed place where you can perform this ritual without interruptions. Arrange your tools and ingredients on a small table or altar.

Anoint the white candle with lavender oil, focusing on your intent to transform your appearance.

Light the white candle and place it in front of you. The white candle symbolizes purity and transformation.

On the piece of parchment, write down the specific features and traits of the person you wish to appear as. Fold the parchment and place it under the bowl of water.

Take the hand mirror and hold it in your hand. Gaze deeply into your reflection, imagining the new appearance you desire.

As you gaze into the mirror, hold the clear quartz in your other hand and chant the following incantation three times:

"Mirror bright, reflect and show,
Transform my face, let changes flow.
By candle's light and crystal clear,
Let a new visage now appear.
Features change, and form anew,
As I will, this spell imbue.
Shape and shift, my face transform,
A different person now is born.
This is my will, so mote it be,
A new reflection, come to me."

Add the fresh mint leaves to the bowl of water. Dip your fingers into the water and gently splash your face, symbolizing the refreshing and transformative power of the mint.

Allow the candle to burn down completely, letting its energy infuse the spell. Once the candle is finished, keep the parchment and clear quartz as talismans of your transformation.

Repeat this ritual as needed to maintain the illusion of the different appearance. Embrace the new traits and features in your daily interactions.

Appear Older

By calling on the wisdom and dignity connected with age, this glamorous spell is meant to produce the illusion of age, therefore enabling you to seem older than you are.

REQUIREMENTS:

❀ A small hand mirror
❀ A grey candle
❀ A piece of parchment
❀ A black pen
❀ Lavender oil
❀ A sprig of rosemary
❀ A bowl of water

INSTRUCTIONS:

Find a quiet and undisturbed place where you can perform this ritual without interruptions. Arrange your tools and ingredients on a small table or altar.

Anoint the grey candle with lavender oil, focusing on your intent to appear older and wiser.

Light the grey candle and place it in front of the mirror. The grey candle symbolizes the wisdom and maturity you wish to project.

On the piece of parchment, write down the specific aspects of aging you wish to embody, such as wisdom, experience, and dignity. Fold the parchment and place it under the candle.

Hold the small hand mirror in one hand and the sprig of rosemary in the other. Gaze deeply into your reflection, focusing on the changes you wish to see.

As you gaze into the mirror, chant the following incantation three times:

"By candle's light and rosemary's grace,
Show in my features an older face.
Wisdom and years, let them appear,
Make me look older, strong and clear.
With each breath and each new dawn,
My youthful looks will be withdrawn.
This is my will, so mote it be,
Age and wisdom, come to me."

Dip the sprig of rosemary into the bowl of water and gently sprinkle your face with the water, symbolizing the flow of time and the changes you wish to see.

Allow the candle to burn down completely, letting its energy infuse the spell. Once the candle is finished, keep the parchment in a safe place as a reminder of your intention.

Repeat this ritual as needed to maintain the illusion of age. Focus on embodying the wisdom and maturity you wish to project in your daily life.

Appear Taller & Increase in Height

This powerful glamour spell is designed to stretch and shape your energy system, making you appear taller. Over time, with constant application, it can lead to genuine physical changes in height.

REQUIREMENTS:

❀ A mirror (optional, for visualization)

INSTRUCTIONS:

Find a quiet and undisturbed place where you can perform this ritual without interruptions. Arrange yourself comfortably in front of a mirror if using one.

Begin by getting a sense of the shape of your energy system (aura) as it is now. Close your eyes and visualize your aura surrounding you.

Take deep breaths, allowing energy to flow into you from above and below. Visualize your aura "inflating" to a larger size. Shape it into a taller, more expansive form, while keeping it balanced and strong.

As you breathe deeply, shape your aura into a taller, more elevated form. Ensure it remains wide and balanced, avoiding a tall and skinny appearance. Visualize yourself growing in height, standing taller and more confident.

Hold this new shape in your mind and let the energies spiral around and through this new form. Chant the following incantation:

"Energy flow, rise and grow,
Lift me up, let height bestow.
Stretch and expand, strong and bright,
Make me taller by day and night."

Hold this visualization steady while continuing to breathe deeply. Focus on your intention without straining, allowing your attention to naturally maintain the new shape.

Practice this exercise as often as possible to communicate your desire to the universe. Consistency is key to letting the powers know your intention to grow into this new shape.

After a few days of practice, you will notice it becomes easier to maintain the visualization. You will start feeling brighter, stronger, taller, and more powerful. Embrace these feelings and let them enhance your confidence and presence.

Appearance Change Spell

This spell is meant to progressively alter your look across time. Regular saying the spell every morning helps you to use your will to produce the intended metamorphosis.

REQUIREMENTS:

❖ A mirror

INSTRUCTIONS:

Find a quiet and undisturbed place where you can perform this ritual without interruptions. Ensure you have a mirror placed in front of you.

Each morning, stand in front of the mirror. Take a few deep breaths to center yourself and clear your mind of distractions.

Visualize the specific change you want to see in your appearance. See it clearly in your mind's eye as if it has already happened.

With a strong and confident voice, chant the following incantation three times:

> "By the power of three, come to me,
> Transform my looks as I decree.
> Let my will be clear and bright,
> Change my form by morning light.
> This is my will, so mote it be,
> My desired change, for all to see."

As you chant, focus on the mirror and visualize the change taking shape. Believe in the power of your words and the magic within you.

Repeat this ritual every morning, consistently focusing on the specific change you wish to achieve. Patience and persistence are key, as gradual transformation takes time.

Notice the subtle changes in your appearance over time. Trust in the process and embrace the transformation as it unfolds.

Body Transformation

Emphasising one particular area at a time, this strong spell is meant to induce slow changes to your body. Using the components of earth and water can help you to direct your will to change your physical form.

REQUIREMENTS:

❁ Full-length mirror
❁ Quartz crystal
❁ Rocks, dirt, or an earth symbol amulet
❁ A bowl of water

INSTRUCTIONS:

Find a quiet and undisturbed place where you can perform this ritual without interruptions. Arrange your tools and ingredients in front of a full-length mirror.

Stand in front of the full-length mirror with a bowl of water placed directly between you and the mirror. Place the earth element (rocks, dirt, or an earth symbol amulet) into the bowl of water. The earth element symbolizes your body, while the water represents the forces of change.

Take the quartz crystal in your hand and hold it in front of you, staring into the mirror. Focus your intent on the specific aspect of your body you wish to change.

Channel your will through the crystal, visualizing the desired transformation. As you concentrate, say the following incantation:

"As water shapes and changes the eternal earth,
So shall my body be reshaped and given birth.
With this crystal, my will be done,
Transform my form until the goal is won."

Continue to stare into the mirror, seeing the desired changes in your reflection. Feel the energy of the earth and water elements working together to reshape your body.

Trust in the power of the spell and your will to bring about the transformation. Be patient and allow the magic to work gradually.

Perform this spell regularly over a period of weeks. Consistency is key, so do not change the aspect you are focusing on night to night. Stay committed until you achieve the desired results.

Cleansing Beauty Bath

This magical bath spell is meant to cleanse you of negativity, boost your beauty, and help you to relax. It calls for a handcrafted, natural face mask to accentuate the ceremony.

REQUIREMENTS:

❀ A warm bath
❀ A handful of rose petals
❀ A couple of tablespoons of lavender flowers
❀ Lavender oil
❀ A few candles (for ambiance)
❀ Sage or sandalwood or other clearing incense
❀ For the Face Mask:
❀ Quarter of an avocado
❀ A couple of strawberries
❀ 1 tomato
❀ Optional: 1 or 2 garlic cloves (for spots)
❀ Optional: Juice from half a lemon (for aging skin)

PREPARE THE FACE MASK:

Gather the avocado, strawberries, tomato, and any optional ingredients. Add a few rose petals and blend the ingredients into a smooth paste. While blending, visualize golden light infusing the mixture, enhancing its beautifying properties. Set the mixture aside.

PREPARE THE BATH INGREDIENTS:

Set aside seven rose petals. Gently boil the remaining rose petals and lavender flowers, then set them aside.

INSTRUCTIONS:

Cleanse your bathroom by burning sage, sandalwood, or another clearing incense of your choice. Focus on clearing the space of any unwanted energies.

Draw a warm bath. Use a tea strainer to add the boiled lavender and rose mixture to the water, ensuring the petals are caught. Add a few drops of lavender oil and light the candles for ambiance. Add the seven reserved rose petals to the bath.

Get into the bath, relax, and inhale the soothing scents. With each breath, relax your body, then ground and center yourself.

Visualise a brilliant healing white light flowing in from the top of your head, spreading through your entire body, and flushing out any negativity. Feel the light deeply.

Take a couple of rose petals floating in the bath and gently rub them on your face. Chant:

> "Great Venus, with beauty divine,
> Fill me with grace, let my face shine.
> Erzulie, Isis, Hathor, Freya too,
> Bless me with charm, pure and true."

Put on the prepared face mask and relax for at least ten minutes. Allow the mask and the bath to work their magic.

After the mask has set, wash it off while still in the bath or stay a bit longer if desired. Feel the beauty and tranquility within.

Conclude the ritual by thanking the Goddess you invoked for her blessings and grace.

Egyptian Beauty Spell

By calling the Goddess of attractiveness, Hathor, or another deity of your choice, this ancient spell is meant to improve your attractiveness by use of a hand mirror and a unique herbal concoction, so capturing the divine spirit of beauty and changing your look.

REQUIREMENTS:

- Hand mirror, never used by you
- 1/4 cup of Vervain
- A pinch of Eyebright
- A pinch of Yerba Santa leaves
- 1/4 cup of spring water
- A piece of red velvet to wrap the mirror
- Chalice
- Athame (ritual knife)

PREPARATION

Perform this spell under a waxing or full moon to harness the moon's growing energy.

INSTRUCTIONS:

Find a quiet and undisturbed place where you can perform this ritual without interruptions. Arrange your tools and ingredients on a small table or altar.

In your chalice, mix the Vervain, Eyebright, Yerba Santa leaves, and spring water. Stir the mixture with your Athame while singing the Song For Beauty.

Paint the mirror with this potion, taking care not to catch your own reflection. The mirror should only capture the essence of the deity or the person you wish to resemble.

36

Stand before the mirror and capture the reflection of Hathor, the Goddess of Beauty, or any other form of beauty you desire. Wrap the mirror in the red velvet cloth.

Take the wrapped mirror to a starlit river or lake. Wait until the surface is calm and still.

Unwrap the mirror and look at your reflection in the water. When ready, cast the mirror into the water, shattering your reflection. As you do this, chant:

> "Aphrodite, born of sea,
> Let thy power transfigure me.
> Grant to me thy rounded breast,
> Slender limbs and all that's best.
> Hair and eyes and nose and chin,
> Smooth, unwrinkled, silken skin.
> To catch the eye and turn the head,
> Of any whom I wish to wed.
> For none can proof against the arts,
> That through his eyes reach to his heart.
> O Goddess of the form divine,
> Make my appearance like to thine!"

Upon the shore, perform a dance in honor of Hathor-Aphrodite, or sing songs of beauty to the stars, celebrating your new-found allure.

Feel the divine energy infusing you with beauty. Trust in the power of the spell to enhance your appearance and confidence.

The line "Of any whom I wish to wed" can be personalized to suit your intentions, such as "Of him whom I desire to wed" or "Of lovers I desire to bed."

Enchantment of Beauty

This magic not only accentuates your exterior beauty but also radiates your inner charm. It is well recognised to reduce flaws and defects, thereby leaving you with a brilliant and harmonic presence.

REQUIREMENTS:

❖ One rose bloom (any color, though white is preferred)
❖ A stove
❖ A boiling pot
❖ Rainwater (approximately two cups)
❖ A small picture of yourself
❖ Salt
❖ One white candle
❖ One large bowl

INSTRUCTIONS:

Collect approximately two cups of rainwater, symbolizing purity and natural renewal.

Find a quiet and undisturbed place where you can perform this ritual. Arrange your tools and ingredients on a small table or altar.

Start by boiling the rainwater on the stove. Once it reaches a rolling boil, break apart the rose bloom's petals and toss them into the pot. White roses work best, but any color will suffice.

Allow the petals to simmer in the water for about five to ten minutes. While they are simmering, place your picture at the bottom of the large bowl. Use the salt to create a circle around the picture, symbolizing protection and sanctity.

Light the white candle and place it beside the bowl, representing purity and illumination.

Carefully pour the boiling water with rose petals into the bowl, covering your picture with the mixture. As you do this, chant:

"Rain from the sky, flower from the earth,
Bestow upon me beauty and worth."

Hold the candle and say:

"Blemishes, I command you to flee,
Beauty's light, envelop me.
As I will it, so shall it be,
My wish fulfilled, let all see."

Dip the candle into the bowl to extinguish the flame, sealing the spell.

For added potency, cover your entire body with the water from the bowl, allowing the petals and picture to remain inside. Let the water dry naturally on your skin.

After **24** hours, burn each rose petal until they are reduced to ash. This act releases your wish and intentions into the universe, hastening the spell's effect.

Once the petals are burned, you may also burn the picture, ensuring it is fully dried. This completes the ritual and solidifies the spell.

Eternal Beauty Spell

Combining the elemental powers of water, fire, and earth, this magical spell is meant to call out lifetime beauty. Using the reflected qualities of the mirror with the force of the rose will help you to let your inner beauty blossom outside.

REQUIREMENTS:

❀ 1 wine glass of water
❀ 1 pinch of salt
❀ 1 red candle
❀ 1 light blue candle
❀ 1 red rose (perfect, without scars or imperfections)
❀ 1 round hand-held mirror

INSTRUCTIONS:

Find a quiet and undisturbed place where you can perform this ritual without interruptions. Arrange your tools and ingredients on a small table or altar.

Using a small knife or a pin, carve the symbol of sex (male or female) into the red candle and a mirror symbol (circle) into the light blue candle.

Drop the pinch of salt into the wine glass of water, saying:

"Beauty be within me,
Beauty now set me free."

Light the light blue candle first, followed by the red candle. Place the candles on either side of the mirror.

Lay the round hand-held mirror between the two candles. Gaze deeply into your reflection, focusing on your inner beauty and visualizing it manifesting outward.

Gently pluck the petals from the red rose, dropping them one by one onto the mirror. As you do this, chant:

"Petals of red, soft and fair,
Beauty flows from everywhere.
In this mirror, let it shine,
Beauty eternal, now is mine."

Once all the petals are placed, drink the water from the glass, saying:

"Beauty, beauty come to me,
Beauty, beauty set me free."

Allow the candles to burn down completely, letting their energy infuse the spell.

Feel the power of the spell enhancing your beauty from within, reflecting in your appearance and aura.

Everlasting Youth

By using the full moon and natural components, this charm is meant to call forth everlasting youth. Through deliberate intent and respect, this ceremny will help you to access the energies to revitalise and replenish.

REQUIREMENTS:

❀ A black candle
❀ A chalice of water
❀ Salt
❀ Two spoonfuls of Vervain
❀ A piece of petrified wood

Timing:

Perform this spell on the night of a full moon to maximize its potency.

INSTRUCTIONS:

Find a quiet and undisturbed outdoor location where you can perform this ritual under the light of the full moon. Arrange your tools and ingredients on a small table or altar.

Light the black candle, focusing on its flame. This represents the transformation and renewal you seek.

Fill the chalice with water and add a pinch of salt, symbolizing purification. Then, add two spoonfuls of Vervain, which represents healing and youth.

Mix the ingredients thoroughly and dip the piece of petrified wood into the chalice. This stone symbolizes strength and endurance.

Pass the petrified wood through the flame of the candle and chant the following incantation:

"Candle, herb, rock, water, salt,
Hear my plea as I exalt.
Age is not what I desire,
It is youth to which I aspire.
Candle, herb, rock, water, salt,
Let my years now come to halt."

Repeat the ritual and chant seven times. With each repetition, touch the rock in turn to the following points on your body: one foot, one hand, one shoulder, the crown of your head, and then down the other side to shoulder, hand, and foot. Visualize the rejuvenating energy flowing into you with each touch.

Once the spell is complete, take the petrified wood immediately to the nearest river, beach, or stream and throw it into the water. This act releases the energy into the natural flow, carrying your intent into the universe.

Eye Colour Change

A ritual of transformation, illusion, and glamour magic

Instead of physically changing the pigment, this spell uses glamour magic to change the way others—including yourself—see your eye colour. This lets the new hue grab hold by energy projection and visualisation.

REQUIREMENTS:

❀ 1 orange candle (Symbolizing transformation, confidence, and change)

❀ 1 pink candle (Symbolizing self-love, beauty, and attraction)

❀ A quiet night (Preferably under a full or waxing moon for growth and enhancement)

❀ A small mirror (To focus the energy into your reflection)

❀ A bowl of water (To absorb and reflect the new energy)

❀ A pinch of chamomile or rose petals (For beauty and softening the change)

❀ A quartz crystal (To amplify the glamour spell)

INSTRUCTIONS:

Find a quiet, undisturbed space where you will not be interrupted. Set your materials in front of you in a circle formation, with the bowl of water in the center.

Arrange the candles—place the orange candle to the right (for transformation) and the pink candle to the left (for beauty and acceptance). Light them, focusing on the flame as the spark of your magic.

Hold the quartz crystal in your hand, feeling its energy attuning to your intention. Gently place it in the water, allowing it to charge the liquid with energy.

Sprinkle the chamomile or rose petals into the water, whispering:

> "Glimmer and gleam, shift and flow,
> Through the veil, let color show."

Close your eyes and breathe deeply, centering your thoughts.

Envision your current eye color in your mind's eye. Let it appear as a radiant glow, surrounding your eyes like an aura.

Slowly begin to shift the hue, seeing the old color fade away like mist. Picture the new color flowing in like liquid light, filling the space and taking root.

Open your eyes and gaze into the mirror, watching your reflection as if it were already transformed.

Chant the following spell aloud three times:

> "Eyes of flame, eyes of sea,
> Shift and change, become of me.
> By will, by sight, by magic's light,
> Reflect my truth, reveal my might."

Repeat this visualization process two more times, each time strengthening the clarity and conviction of the transformation.

Dip your fingers into the charged water and gently dab it around your eyes, sealing the energy with a final whisper:

> "What was, now fades. What is, remains.
> As I see it, so it shall be."

Blow out the candles, thanking the fire for aiding your transformation.

Leave the bowl of water under moonlight overnight to carry the residual energy into the next day.

Throughout the day, reaffirm your new eye color in your mind. When you look into a mirror, picture them as they should be, reinforcing the glamour spell.

Eye Colour Transformation

This glamour spell allows you to change the look of your eye color through focused vision. By visualising your face as a mask and filling the eyeholes with the desired color, you can enchant your eyes to reflect the new hue.

REQUIREMENTS:

✿ Incense (optional, for relaxation)

INSTRUCTIONS:

Find a comfortable place where you will not be distracted. Light some incense if it helps you relax and focus your mind.

Sit comfortably and clear your mind of any distractions. Focus on the color you want your eyes to become.

Imagine your face as a mask that you are holding about five inches away from your eyes. Visualize a light, like a flashlight, shining through the eyeholes of the mask.

Start with the light dim and gradually make it brighter. The light should be the color you want your eyes to look. Hold this image as long as you can, seeing the eyeholes of the mask fill up with the desired color.

Visualize yourself putting the mask on and absorbing it into your skin. As you do this, imagine your eyes becoming the new color. Feel the transformation taking place within you.

Once the visualization is complete, take a deep breath and open your eyes. If you used incense, allow its calming scent to seal the transformation.

The spell's effect lasts about an hour and a half. For longer durations, perform a quick touch-up visualization, similar to refreshing makeup, by visualizing a quick zap of the desired color in a mirror.

<u>NOTES</u>

Feminine Beauty Spell

Designed especially for girls and ladies, this spell enhances beauty, strength, and ability. Calling the Goddess helps you to access her divine energy to change and strengthen yourself.

INSTRUCTIONS:

Find a quiet and undisturbed place where you can perform this ritual without interruptions. Ensure you are calm and centered, ready to connect with the divine.

Close your eyes and visualize the Goddess showering you with love, light, and beauty. Feel her energy enveloping you, filling you with her divine grace and power.

As you visualize, recite the following incantation with clear intention and focus:

"O Lady of shimmering beauty bright,
For whom stars are jewels in the night,
Universe your creation, your playful art,
Weaver of destinies, protector of the heart.
Make me now, your daughter true,
One with thee, in all I do.
Grant me power, strong and vast,
Strength within, unsurpassed.
As eternal as the boundless sea,
Assured of my powers, let me be.
Winds, waters, fires, and hills,
Lend their might to my will.
Wisdom of ages, lore of eons past,
Knowledge of light, knowledge of dark, steadfast.
Grant me beauty, ever more divine,
Reflecting thee, let me shine.
Build magick within, power profound,

48

Make me greater, in strength unbound.
O Goddess, my friend and mother,
I give you thanks, like no other.
May this magic, strong and pure,
Return to me, ever sure.
Wisdom, strength, comeliness, and compassion,
Grow within, in endless fashion.
So mote it be!"

As you chant, feel the energy of the Goddess infusing you with her strength and beauty. Allow this divine power to settle within you, enhancing your abilities and self-assurance.

Thank the Goddess for her blessings and gently bring yourself back to the present moment. Open your eyes and feel the transformation within you.

Regularly connect with the Goddess through visualization and chanting to maintain and enhance the spell's effects.

Glamour and Beauty

This magical charm calls the goddess of love and beauty, therefore enhancing your beauty and brilliance. Through committed attention, this ritual will help you to acquire the divine appeal and charm of the goddess.

REQUIREMENTS:

❂ Roses
❂ Damiana
❂ Ginger
❂ Dong quai
❂ Coriander
❂ Primrose flowers
❂ Green glass jar
❂ Lovage roots
❂ Rose petals
❂ Musk oil
❂ Pink candle
❂ Venus oil or rose oil or perfume
❂ Aura of Enchantment Incense
❂ Small mirror

PREPARATION:

Perform this spell on a Friday night, the day sacred to Venus, the goddess of love and beauty.

INSTRUCTIONS:

Mix the dry herbs of roses, Damiana, ginger, Dong quai, coriander, and primrose flowers. Place the mixture in a green glass jar and set it on your altar.

On the night of Venus, prepare a bath with lovage roots and rose petals. Soak in the bath, absorbing the herbs' essence. Afterward, dry yourself and anoint your skin with musk oil, infusing your body with its enchanting scent.

Go to your altar nude. Light a pink candle anointed with Venus oil, rose oil, or your favorite perfume. Burn Aura of Enchantment Incense to fill the space with its mystical aroma.

Place a small mirror on the altar. Gaze deeply into your reflection and recite the following incantation:

"Soft, my skin, as Diana's grace,
Smoldering eyes, Aradia's face.
Sensuous as a Goddess bright,
Transform my beauty in this night.
Figures of fire that shift and change,
Shape me now, let beauty reign.
Blessed by the Goddess of Love,
Shine my charm, as stars above."

Perform this ritual each night for seven nights, leaving the tea mixture on the altar until the spell is complete.

After the seven nights, drink a cup of the herbal tea daily and wash your face with rose water upon waking to maintain the spell's energy.

As you continue to use the tea and rose water, embrace the beauty and confidence bestowed upon you by the goddess.

Glamour and Beauty 2

This glamour spell is designed to enhance your beauty and radiance by calling the forces of the West and the element of Water. Performing this ritual under a Full Moon or on a Friday during the Waxing Moon will magnify its benefits.

REQUIREMENTS:

❁ A bowl of spring water
❁ Herbs for beauty (such as lavender and catnip)
❁ A white rose, separated from the stem
❁ A mirror

PREPARATION:

The best time to perform this spell is during the Full Moon or on a Friday during the Waxing Moon.

Instructions:

Before beginning the spell, take a ritual bath or perform a purification ritual to cleanse your body and spirit, creating a fresh slate for the magic to work.

Cast a circle and find a quiet, undisturbed place where you can perform the ritual. Ensure you are calm and centered.

Sit or stand facing the West. Pour the spring water into the bowl and hold it up towards the western direction. Say:

"I hail to the West and the forces of Water,
Hear and aid me in this magic hour.
Grant me your beauty, let it shine bright,
Shape and form me in this night."

Set the white rose petals on top of the water. Gently stir the water three times clockwise with your fingers. As you do this, say:

> "With harm towards none, and for the free will of all,
> Let beauty and love upon me fall.
> Radiate with self-love, I shine,
> By the power of water, I am divine."

Take the rose petals out of the water and hold them in your hands. Say:

> "By the powers of the West,
> The forces of Water,
> I charge this flower with love and grace.
> Beauty is here, it shines with power,
> Beauty is here, contained in this flower."

Place the charged flower in a box along with catnip and/or lavender to keep it as a reminder of your true beauty. If a friend or loved one needs the power of love and beauty, share the story of the rose and give them the flower to continue its magic.

Thank the forces of the West and the element of Water for their assistance. Close your circle and ground yourself.

Keep the flower in its box and revisit it whenever you need a reminder of your inner and outer beauty. Share its power with others in need.

Glamourous Beauty

This magical glamour spell is meant to accentuate your features and make you seem to others brilliant. Using the energies of rose quartz and rose petals and calling upon Venus's strength can help you to mirror your inner beauty in your appearance.

REQUIREMENTS:

❀ One rose quartz crystal
❀ Six rose petals
❀ A small bottle of witch hazel
❀ A mirror

INSTRUCTIONS:

Find a quiet and undisturbed place where you can perform this ritual without interruptions. Arrange your tools and ingredients on a small table or altar.

Look at your face in the mirror and acknowledge any flaws or imperfections. Visualize your face transforming into the ideal image you desire.

Gently rub the rose quartz crystal over the problem areas on your face. As you do this, chant:

> "Stone of beauty, stone of love,
> Erase imperfections as I rub.
> Bring to me the face I see,
> As I will, so mote it be."

Open the bottle of witch hazel and insert the rose quartz crystal into it.

Take the six rose petals in your right hand and say:

"Venus, Goddess of beauty rare,
I offer you these petals fair.
Bless them with your loveliness,
And bring the beauty I request."

Rub the rose petals over any lines, wrinkles, or imperfections on your face. Then drop the petals into the bottle of witch hazel.

Cap the bottle tightly and give it six good shakes each day for a week.

At the end of the week, use the witch hazel mixture as a toner after washing your face every day. As you apply it, say:

"Imperfections, go away,
Beauty of Venus, come forth this day."

Feel the enchanting energy of Venus and the rose quartz enhancing your beauty. Trust in the power of the spell to reveal your inner radiance.

Irresistible Beauty Spell

By calling on the components of earthiness and heat and using a nice bath, you can access the magic to radiate beauty from within and improve your attractiveness and make you desirable.

REQUIREMENTS:

❀ Brand-new bath oil or body wash
(lavender, jasmine, musk, or ylang-ylang scent)
❀ One carrot, chopped into three pieces
❀ Three small orange candles

INSTRUCTIONS:

Perform this spell on a Tuesday night in your bathroom. This day is associated with Mars, symbolizing strength and attraction.

Draw a super-hot bath, using double the amount of bath oil or body wash you usually use. Allow the steam to fog up the mirror.

With your fingertip, write your name followed by "is the BOMB!" on the fogged-up mirror. This affirms your intent and channels the energy towards you.

Chop the carrot into three pieces and float them in the bathwater, symbolizing earthiness and nourishment.

Light the three small orange candles around the bath. Do not get into the bath yet; it's still too hot.

Stand by the bath and chant the following incantation three times:

"In this water from the heat,
Bathe me now, head to feet.
With warmth and scent, I am complete,
Irresistible beauty, my charm's retreat."

Once the bath has cooled to a comfortable temperature, step in and relax. Breathe in the scented bath oil or body wash, allowing the aroma to envelop you. Soak for at least 20 minutes.

After your bath, blow out the candles. Allow the candle wax to cool before handling them.

Take the three pieces of carrot and bury them outside. This symbolizes grounding the spell and returning the energy to the earth.

Use the same scented bath oil or body wash in your daily showers or baths to maintain the spell's energy and enhance your beauty.

Self Image Spell

This spell is designed to boost your self-image and nurture self-love by connecting with the principle of beauty and the Goddess of Beauty in one of her many incarnations. By utilising pink candles and love oil, you evoke a sense of love and appreciation for yourself.

REQUIREMENTS:

❀ At least one pink candle (more if you prefer)

❀ A handheld mirror

❀ Love oil

INSTRUCTIONS:

Find a quiet and undisturbed place where you can perform this ritual without interruptions. Arrange your tools and ingredients on a small table or altar.

Anoint the pink candle(s) with love oil, working towards you to draw in the qualities of self-love and beauty. Focus on your ideal qualities of beauty as you do so.

Light the pink candle(s) and place them in front of you. Hold the hand-held mirror and stare deeply into it, first seeing the person you are now.

Close your eyes and visualize the changes you desire in your self-image. See yourself as the person you wish to be, radiating beauty and confidence.

Open your eyes, look into the mirror, and recite the following incantation out loud:

"Sacred flame, as you dance,
Call upon my sacred glance.
Call upon my better self,
Grant me beauty, love, and health.
Blessed flame, shining bright,
Bring about these changes night by night.
Give me now my second chance,
My beauty and glamour, please enhance.
Power of three, let it be seen,
Let my beauty now be gleaned."

Spend a few moments meditating on your new self-image, allowing the positive energy to infuse your being. Affirm your beauty and self-worth with each breath.

Snuff out the candle (do not blow it out) and relight it the next night, burning it for at least an hour. Repeat the incantation three times each night to reinforce the spell.

Recognize and embrace your inner beauty, allowing it to shine through in your daily life. This spell helps you project that inner beauty outward, making it evident to others.

Spell for Clear Skin

This spell is designed to cleanse and clarify your skin by summoning the natural healing properties of apples and the blessings of the Goddess. By using both half of the apples and singing incantations, you can remove blemishes and promote a healthy skin.

REQUIREMENTS:

❖ Two apples
❖ A knife

INSTRUCTIONS:

Find a quiet and undisturbed place where you can perform this ritual without interruptions. Arrange your tools and ingredients on a small table or altar.

Take one apple and cut it horizontally across the middle. When you cut it, you will see a five-pointed star. Hold the apple half and focus on its natural healing energy.

Rub one half of the apple over your face or the affected area. As you do this, chant:

> "Apple, sacred fruit of the Goddess,
> With this gift, I do caress.
> The pimple that brought me shame,
> I banish this zit in your name."

Take the second apple and cut it vertically from top to bottom. Hold one half and focus on its purifying properties.

Rub this half of the apple over your face or the affected area. As you do this, chant:

"I love and accept myself as I am today,
Clear skin I summon to come my way.
By my will, so mote it be,
Three times three, so shall it be."

Bury the first apple half by a tree, bush, or flower outside.

Bury the second apple half by a body of water. If you cannot find a suitable place, bury it anywhere and pour water over it, symbolizing purification.

Close the ritual by thanking the Goddess for her assistance and the natural elements for their healing powers.

The Mental "Notice Me"

This mental magic is meant to draw in a certain individual. It guarantees respect of their free choice by planting a suggestion in their head instead of dictating their behaviour.

INSTRUCTIONS:

Find a quiet and undisturbed place where you can concentrate without interruptions. Sit comfortably and relax.

Take a few deep breaths to center yourself. Clear your mind of any distractions and prepare to focus solely on the person whose attention you seek.

Close your eyes and bring a clear image of the person to mind. See them vividly, imagining their presence and energy.

Concentrate on your desire to get their attention. Feel the intention building within you, becoming stronger with each breath.

Mentally repeat the following spell, focusing on each word and its meaning:

> "Within my mind, this spell I weave,
> To make it known, I seek to achieve.
> Notice me, come speak my name,
> Show your interest, ignite the flame."

As you chant, visualize the person turning towards you, smiling, and making an effort to approach you. Feel the connection forming in your mind.

Once you have repeated the incantation several times and feel the intention is strong, release the visualization and trust that the spell has been set in motion.

Throughout the day, maintain a positive and open attitude, allowing the energy of the spell to flow naturally.

True Beauty

This magical spell is meant to accentuate and expose your actual beauty—inner as much as outside. Connecting with the ground and tending a plant helps you to match your development with the cycles of the soil, therefore enabling your beauty to blossom.

REQUIREMENTS:

❀ A dish full of good, fertile soil
❀ A yellow candle
❀ A full-sized mirror
❀ Olive, patchouli, jasmine, or cinnamon essential oil
❀ A small flower pot
❀ A flower or plant seed

INSTRUCTIONS:

Find a quiet and undisturbed place where you can perform this ritual without interruptions. Arrange your tools and ingredients on a small table or altar.

Anoint the yellow candle with the essential oil of your choice, focusing on your intent to enhance and reveal your beauty.

Place the anointed candle in the center of the dish of soil. Ensure the soil is fertile and not dry or dusty.

Light the yellow candle and sit down with it positioned between you and the mirror.

Look deeply into your reflection in the mirror. Without vanity, contemplate the aspects of yourself you find most beautiful, both physically and mentally. Focus on your inner beauty and your outer beauty, appreciating all that you are.

As you gaze into the mirror, chant the following incantation three times:

"Mirror bright, reflect to me,
Inner beauty, let it be.
Outer grace, I now embrace,
Beauty shines from every place."

Perform this ritual for three consecutive nights. Allow the candle to burn down completely each night.

Once the entire candle has burnt down, remove the wax from the dish. Place the soil from the dish into a small flower pot and plant a seed inside it. Water and care for the seed, nurturing it to grow.

As you tend to the plant, know that your beauty will grow and flourish just as the plant emerges from its seed. Your inner and outer beauty will shine brighter than ever before.

It is crucial to maintain positive thoughts, focusing on the beauty you already possess. Do not think of what needs to change, but rather appreciate your existing beauty.

Ugly Spell

This charm is meant to make your hated individual less appealing. Under the full moon, you can symbolically change the look of earth and fire by combining their elements.

REQUIREMENTS:

❁ Mud
❁ A picture of the person you wish to affect
❁ A black candle
❁ A pot of water
❁ Full moon night

PREPARATION

Perform this spell on the night of a full moon to enhance its potency.

INSTRUCTIONS:

Find a quiet and undisturbed place where you can perform this ritual under the full moon. Arrange your tools and ingredients on a small table or altar.

Light the black candle, focusing on its flame. This represents the transformation you seek.

Place the pot of water nearby. Ensure the candle can stand in the water without falling over and extinguishing.

Hold the picture of the person in your hands. Look at it and visualize them becoming less attractive. Chant the following incantation:

"Under the moon's full light,
By this spell, I change your sight.
Day by day, ugliness grow,
Until my will lets it go."

Spread the mud over the picture, covering the person's face. As you do this, chant:

"Mud of earth, conceal and blight,
Change this face, hide from sight."

Set the picture on fire using the candle flame. Hold it over the pot of water, and say:

"Fire burn, the visage mar,
By my will, now and far."

Once the face is burned, drop the picture into the water to extinguish the flame. Say:

"Water cool, extinguish fast,
This spell is cast, their beauty past."

Clean up all materials. Throw the picture and the used materials into the trash. Take the trash out immediately to remove the remnants from your space.

Vervain Youth Charm

This charm is meant to accentuate and extend your young vitality. Doing this ceremony beneath the full moon can help you to harness the natural energy to revitalise your body and spirit.

REQUIREMENTS:

❁ One black candle
❁ One chalice (or glass/metal cup)
❁ Salt
❁ Two spoonfuls of Vervain
❁ A piece of petrified wood
❁ A small rock

Timing:

Perform this spell on the night of a full moon to maximize its potency.

INSTRUCTIONS:

Find a quiet and undisturbed outdoor location where you can perform this ritual under the light of the full moon. Arrange your tools and ingredients on a small table or altar.

Light the black candle, focusing on its flame. This represents transformation and renewal.

Fill the chalice with water, then add a pinch of salt and two spoonfuls of Vervain. Mix thoroughly, symbolizing purification and the essence of youth.

Dip the piece of petrified wood into the chalice, infusing it with the mixture's rejuvenating properties.

Pass the rock through the flame of the candle and chant the following incantation with intent and focus:

"Candle, herb, rock, water, salt,
Hear me as my song exalts.
Age is not my heart's desire,
It is youth to which I aspire.
Candle, herb, rock, water, salt,
Grant me youth, this night exalt."

Repeat the ritual and chant seven times. With each repetition, touch the rock to the following points on your body: one foot, one hand, one shoulder, the crown of your head, then down the other side to the opposite shoulder, hand, and foot. Visualize the rejuvenating energy flowing into you with each touch.

Once the spell is complete, take the rock immediately to the nearest river, beach, or stream and throw it into the water. This act releases the energy into the natural flow, carrying your intent into the universe.

Books by this Author

- The Protection Bible - The Essential Book of Protection Spells and Magic
- The Essential Book of Binding Spells and Magic
- The Essential Book of Cleansing, Blessing, and Purification Spells and Magic
- The Essential Book of Healing Spells and Magic
- The Essential Book of Household Spells and Magic
- The Essential Book of Love Spells and Magic

More Books by Erebus Society

The Standard Book of Candle Magic
by K.P. Theodore

In The Standard Book of Candle Magic you will learn about the use of candles in magical traditions, the meanings of colours so you can create your own candle magic rituals, how to prepare for magical practice, how to cast a standard circle, and over 30 Candle Magic spells for your everyday magical needs.

The Standard Book of Meditation
by K.P. Theodore

Within the pages of this book, you will find a diverse array of meditation techniques waiting to be explored. From breath awareness to body scan, loving-kindness to visualization, the author has meticulously assembled a rich tapestry of practices that invite you to embark on a transformative inner journey.

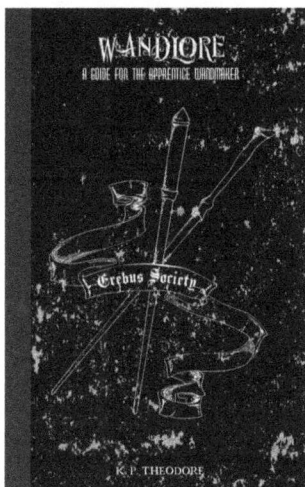

Wandlore –
A Guide for the Apprentice Wandmaker
by K.P. Theodore

Delve into the ancient and intricate art of wandmaking with this comprehensive guide to the origins, properties, and crafting of magick wands. This book serves as both an introduction to wandlore and a hands-on manual for those who aspire to become skilled wand makers.

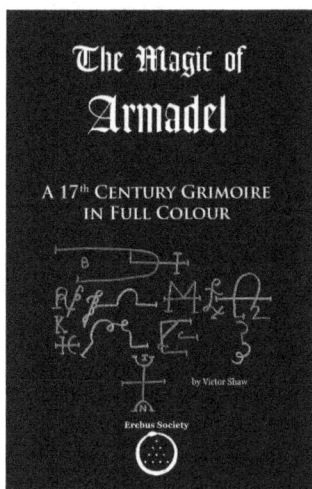

The Magic of Armadel – A 17th Century Grimoire in Full Colour
by Victor Shaw

The Grimoire of Armadel is a book of Celestial Magick and contains information, seals, and sigils of Angels, Demons and other Celestial Spirits.

It is classed as a Christian/Theistic Grimoire, and it was first translated by S.L. McGregor Mathers in the late 1890's from the original French and Latin manuscript that can be found in the Biblotheque l'Arsenal in Paris.

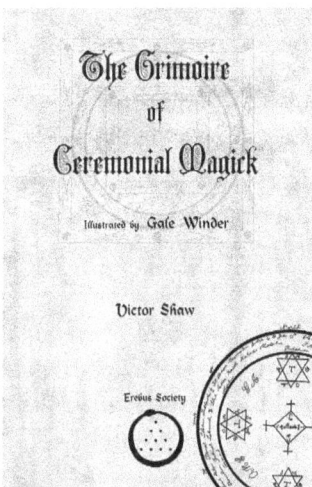

The Grimoire of Ceremonial Magick
by Victor Shaw

This book is a collection of passages, rites, practices, and rituals from various famous Grimoires. It is a cluster of the most obscure and powerful invocations, ceremonies, and pacts, and it explains their history and origins while it refutes certain myths surrounding Ancient Grimoires, and discusses the theology therein.

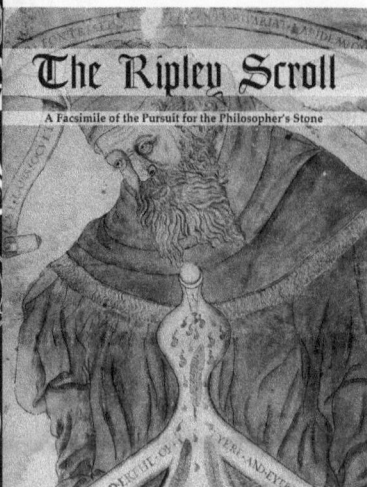

The Ripley Scroll: A Facsimile of the Pursuit for the Philosopher's Stone
by Victor Shaw

The 'Ripley scroll' or 'Ripley Scrowle' is a paramount alchemical work of the 15th century as it depicts the mystical and laborious process for the pursuit of the Philosopher's Stone. A legendary substance that can turn base metals into gold and can also be used in the making of the elixir of life, providing its possessor with prolonged life or even Immortality.

The Fundamental Book of Sigil Magick
by K.P. Theodore

This book serves as a textbook for those who wish to study the art of Sigil Magick. In its pages you will find information about the different kinds of sigils, their use, activation techniques and how to create custom tailored sigils from scratch.

Learn how to captivate emotions, empower the mind, create mental barriers, re-program the brain and alter consciousness by the use of "Mental Sigils".

The Accelerated Necromancer
by Gavin Fox

Necromancy has long been misunderstood, reduced to taboo and superstition. In this insightful work, Gavin redefines the practice, blending witchcraft and chaos magick to offer a responsible, spiritually enriching path.

With practical techniques, seasonal rites, and a fresh take on working with the dead, this book is a must-read for those seeking to walk the shadows with wisdom and reverence.